G000162139

GOD and COUNTRY
Reflections for Catholics in the Military

Rev. Michael Ortiz
Retired United States Army Colonel and Chaplain

ST. ANTHONY MESSENGER PRESS

Cincinnati, Ohio

Name: _____

Rank: _____

Unit: _____

Scripture passages have been taken from *New Revised Standard Version Bible,* copyright ©1989 by the Division of Christian Education of the National Council of the Churches of Christ in the U.S.A., and used by permission. All rights reserved.

Cover design by Jennifer Tibbits
Book design by Phillips Robinette, O.F.M., and Jennifer Tibbits

LIBRARY OF CONGRESS CATALOGING-IN-PUBLICATION DATA
Ortiz, Michael.
  God and country : reflections for Catholics in the military / Michael Ortiz.
      p. cm.
  Includes bibliographical references.
  ISBN 978-0-86716-577-7 (pbk. : alk. paper) 1. Catholic Church—Prayers
      and devotions. 2. Soldiers—Prayers and devotions. I. Title.
  BX2149.2.O78 2007
  248.8'8—dc22
                                                      2007035460
  ISBN 978-0-86716-577-7

Published by St. Anthony Messenger Press
28 W. Liberty St.
Cincinnati, OH 45202
www.AmericanCatholic.org
Printed in the United States of America.

Printed on acid-free paper.

07 08 09 10 11 5 4 3 2 1

CONTENTS

INTRODUCTION

* * * * *

Anyone in the military is familiar with the field manual, the how-to manual that offers a basic orientation in a specific field or piece of equipment. This booklet is sort of a field manual for the Catholic, because its intent is to offer Catholics serving in the army, air force, navy, marines or coast guard a refresher course on the basic tenets of their faith. My experience has shown that most young Catholics in America today have received little education in the importance of the Bible and the seven sacraments of the church. The format of this manual is arranged so that the topics are based on prayers from the Bible and then a relatively current story in our present day.

The following format is suggested in choosing one of the topics. You can obtain a Bible or New Testament from your chaplain.

- Find a quiet comfortable place (your tent, under a tree or in your Humvee).

- Make the Sign of the Cross and read the Scripture passage carefully, or even open up your Bible and read more of the chapter quoted. Take two to three minutes to reflect on the passage.

- In order to reflect more deeply, read the additional story included with the Scripture passage or perhaps recall a similar story from your own experience.

- Take another minute or two to apply the reflection to your personal life. How much are you informed about the Scripture quote? What does our church teach about this? Should you approach your chaplain about your feelings, or should you write or e-mail your loved ones about your thoughts?

- Take some personal notes. There is space in this booklet to record your personal thoughts, doubts and resolutions.

The above format can be helpful because it's so simple to follow, like your field manual.

READING THE BIBLE

* * * * *

This is the disciple who is testifying to these things and has written them, and we know that his testimony is true. But there are also many other things that Jesus did; if every one of them were written down, I suppose that the world itself could not contain the books that would be written.

—JOHN 21:24–25

Meditation

John's passage was written after the death and resurrection of Jesus. Though he is writing about the life of Jesus, John certainly knew about the prophets of the Old Testament. Are you versed in the entire Bible (Old and New Testaments)? Try getting a Catholic Bible through your chaplain's office and become familiar with it.

Terry Anderson had been a war correspondent with the U.S. Marines during the Vietnam War. He changed jobs and went to work as a reporter for the Associated Press because he felt he had witnessed too much. He was sent to Beirut where he felt safe, that is, until soldiers broke into his home one evening and arrested him. They threw him in jail where he remained for seven years. During his confinement he began praying. He had been raised Catholic, but had not been practicing his faith. While in prison a guard passed him a Bible. Terry began to read it since he had nothing better to do. Through reading and studying, he began to realize what he had been missing. Among the other prisoners was a Catholic priest, Father Martin Jenko, who helped and motivated Terry to renew his faith. Terry Anderson now writes and speaks of his experiences. He attributes his return to faith through the study of that Bible given him by one of the prison guards and his conversations with Father Jenko.

Application

Perhaps you, too, can become a better Christian, and a better believer, if you familiarize yourself with the Bible. Consult your chaplain about how to better understand and appreciate Scripture. Ask for some recommendations for online and print resources to help you expand your knowledge of the Word of God.

Personal Notes:

BAPTISM

* * * * *

Then Jesus came from Galilee to John at the Jordan, to be baptized by him. John would have prevented him, saying, "I need to be baptized by you, and do you come to me?" But Jesus answered him, "Let it be so now; for it is proper for us in this way to fulfill all righteousness." Then he consented. And when Jesus had been baptized, just as he came up from the water, suddenly the heavens were opened to him and he saw the Spirit of God descending like a dove and alighting on him. And a voice from heaven said, "This is my Son, the Beloved, with whom I am well pleased."

—MATTHEW 3:13–17

Meditation

John the Baptist preached conversion—a new commitment to living a godly life—to his people. As a sign of their new commitment, they were baptized. Jesus was baptized at the beginning of his ministry. We Catholics are inaugurated into the church through the sacrament of baptism. Through this baptism we are cleansed from original sin.

Recently we have heard from the media about immigration and citizenship more than ever before. Immigrants flock to our shores seeking a better life and more freedom. Becoming an American citizen certainly entitles us to many benefits. My parents migrated to this country with their parents. They chose to become citizens for the sake of their children. They never regretted this decision because they saw how their children enjoyed freedom, education and advancement in life.

Application

Baptism is the sacrament that has made you a "citizen" of the kingdom of God. This sacrament opens up the freedoms that all humans seek. Have you ever witnessed a baptism or been asked to be a godparent? How did you feel?

Personal Notes:

CONFIRMATION

* * * * *

When the day of Pentecost had come, they were all together in one place. And suddenly from heaven there came a sound like the rush of a violent wind, and it filled the entire house where they were sitting. Divided tongues, as of fire, appeared among them, and a tongue rested on each of them. All of them were filled with the Holy Spirit and began to speak in other languages, as the Spirit gave them ability.

—ACTS 2:1–4

Meditation

The quotation above continues with the account of the apostles laying their hands upon people from every nation under heaven. The ability of the apostles to be understood in different languages is a sign of the special gifts received through their confirmation.

The late Cardinal John O'Connor became archbishop of New York after having served as a navy chaplain and eventually becoming the chief of navy chaplains. As a senior chaplain at Fort Benning, Georgia, I invited the archbishop to administer the sacrament of confirmation to the young Catholic soldiers there. This was perhaps the best confirmation I had ever witnessed. As the soldiers came forward to be anointed and to receive the confirmation names they had chosen, the then-archbishop took the time to ask each what he or she knew about his or her new patron and how best to imitate that saint. Each person confirmed was so impressed by the inspiring words of the archbishop that almost all told me after the ceremony that they really felt they had received something special.

Application

Just as the apostles on the first Pentecost received a special gift from Jesus and just as the soldiers at Fort Benning felt "different," so can you if you have not yet received the sacrament of confirmation. The archbishop and the bishops of our military vicariate visit all U.S. military installations at least once a year for confirmations. If you have not been confirmed, now is the time to contact your Catholic chaplain for more information on the reception of this sacrament.

Personal Notes:

RECONCILIATION

* * * * *

I will give you the keys of the kingdom of heaven, and whatever you bind on earth will be bound in heaven, and whatever you loose on earth will be loosed in heaven.

—MATTHEW 16:19

…Receive the Holy Spirit. If you forgive the sins of any, they are forgiven them; if you retain the sins of any, they are retained.

—JOHN 20:22b–23

Meditation

The sacrament of reconciliation is the confession of one's sins to a priest. It heals the damage sin causes to our relationship with God and one another. When is the last time you went to confession? The priest offers us absolution. It cleans our soul just like water washes the soil off our hands, faces and bodies. We like to stay clean…don't we?

It was their first parachute jump. After three torturous weeks of airborne training, the young soldiers were preparing for their first jump from a C-130 aircraft into the drop zone at Fort Benning, Georgia. As chaplain for the airborne school, I knew what was going through the minds of these young paratroopers-to-be. One Sunday I addressed the Catholics in the group before Mass: "I'll make a deal with you," I said. "I promise to jump with your class on Monday if you promise to go to confession and communion during today's Mass." Needless to say, I was late starting Mass that day because of the many confessions. This proves to me that many Catholics *do* believe in the forgiveness of sins and in being prepared spiritually in the event of a mishap.

Application

Just as the young paratroopers were determined to be prepared, so also must we be prepared in our daily lives. If you are ready for the sacrament of reconciliation, see a Catholic chaplain and seek forgiveness for your sins. "Receive the Holy Spirit."

Personal Notes:

HOLY ORDERS

* * * * *

And Jesus said to them, "Follow me and I will make you
fish for people." And immediately they left their nets
and followed him. As he went a little farther, he saw
James son of Zebedee and his brother John, who were
in their boat mending the nets. Immediately he called
them; and they left their father Zebedee in the boat
with the hired men, and followed him.

—MARK 1:17–20

Meditation

That Christ established priesthood as he began
organizing his church is evident in Scripture. Our
country recognizes the importance of having a
chaplain to minister to people in the military. Take a
few minutes to reflect on what the priesthood means
to you.

Father Emil J. Kapaun, born in Pilsen, Kansas, in 1916,
felt called to the priesthood from childhood. He left
home at a very early age to study at a minor seminary.
In 1944 he volunteered for the U.S. Army Chaplaincy.
After his three-year commitment, he returned to his
diocese and worked in parishes there. A quiet but dedi-
cated individual, he felt compelled to return to his

soldiers when the Korean War broke out in 1948; in 1950 he was sent to Korea. Chaplain Kapaun had been in Korea just a few months when he was captured and listed as a POW. Survivors of the POW camp related what made this priest-chaplain a hero. During the seven months Chaplain Kapaun was a POW, his name became known by every single prisoner as well as the prison guards. The rosary, his missal and his Bible became his tools of ministry. He tended the wounds of the sick and dying regardless of race, color or creed. He scrounged and stole food for the hungry. After seven months of self-sacrificing and ministry, he succumbed to the harsh treatment and died in 1951. His cause for sainthood is being brought to Rome.

Application

Have you ever thought about approaching and becoming familiar with your Catholic chaplain? Do you know his name? He has volunteered for the purpose of ministering to you. Introduce yourself to him when you can. Also, remember your chaplain and all military chaplains in your daily prayer.

Personal Notes:

ANOINTING OF THE SICK

* * * * *

You are the light of the world. A city built on a hill cannot be hidden. No one after lighting a lamp puts it under the bushel basket, but on the lampstand, and it gives light to all in the house. In the same way, let your light shine before others, so that they may see your good works and give glory to your Father in heaven.

—MATTHEW 5:14–16

Meditation

People in the military are more likely to recognize individuals who are outstanding in the performance of their duties. Take a few minutes to explore how the above Scripture quote might relate to their actions.

The Congressional Medal of Honor is the highest military award that our nation offers its heroes for conspicuous gallantry above and beyond the call of duty. One such hero in the Vietnam War was Father Vincent R. Capodanno, a Catholic navy chaplain assigned to the First Marine Division. *The Grunt Padre* is the story of this devoted priest who had been a missionary in Taipei prior to joining the navy. Every marine who met Father Capodanno saw in him a fellow "grunt" who did and suffered as they did. In "Operation Rio Blanco" Father Capodanno rushed to the platoon under heavy attack. He dodged small-arms fire, grenades and mortar rounds to get to wounded men. While anointing them, he was severely wounded on his arms, legs and hands, but he refused to leave his men. Machine-gunfire finally brought him down.

Application

If possible, get a copy of *The Grunt Padre* and read how one man made a difference to soldiers dying in battle. If you cannot get the book, recall someone whose light shone before others, whose good works gave glory to God.

Personal Notes:

MARRIAGE

* * * * *

But from the beginning of creation, "God made them
male and female." "For this reason a man shall leave his
father and mother and be joined to his wife, and the
two shall become one flesh." So they are no longer two,
but one flesh. Therefore what God has joined together,
let no one separate.

—MARK 10:6–9

Meditation

Christ had such esteem for marriage that he graced
the couple of Cana by his presence at the recommen-
dation of Mary, his mother. He performed his first
public miracle there. Married or not, Christians must
respect and uphold the sacredness of this sacrament.

George was the ninth of fourteen children and grew up
in a suburb of Chicago. After he graduated from high
school, his widowed mother couldn't afford to send him
to college. He joined the army with the intention of
saving enough to go to college. He survived the conflict
in Vietnam and returned to the United States, enrolling
in a university in Texas. While there he met, fell in love
with and eventually married a young Texan girl, also a
student. Both came from devout Catholic families.
George was recruited to the FBI upon graduation, while

his wife became a teacher. In just a short while George joined the CIA and spent much of his time overseas in clandestine operations. Though this arrangement was difficult for George, it also left his wife alone to raise and educate their two children. In spite of separation and his dangerous work, he never neglected his obligation as a husband and father. He made sure that his son and daughter received and practiced their Catholic faith. George and his wife, both now retired, have never regretted the sacrifices they have had to make in their marriage and family life because they have seen the result—their two wonderful children.

Application

At a time when so many marriages fail, it might be wise to look into your own life. If you are already married, how is your life in the service affecting your marriage? How are you meeting some of the challenges of separation from your spouse and family? If you are not yet married, how might your self-discipline and military training serve you in married life? How can you support your comrades who are married?

Personal Notes:

DIVORCE

* * * * *

Some Pharisees came to him, and to test him they asked, "Is it lawful for a man to divorce his wife for any cause?" He answered, "Have you not read that the one who made them at the beginning 'made them male and female,' and said, 'For this reason a man shall leave his father and mother and be joined to his wife, and the two shall become one flesh'? So they are no longer two, but one flesh. Therefore what God has joined together, let no one separate." They said to him, "Why then did Moses command us to give a certificate of dismissal and to divorce her?" He said to them, "It was because you were so hard-hearted that Moses allowed you to divorce your wives, but at the beginning it was not so. And I say to you, whoever divorces his wife, except for unchastity, and marries another commits adultery."

—MATTHEW 19:3–9

Meditation

Take a few minutes to reflect on the Scripture passage. Divorce, even among Catholics, has increased dramatically. Admittedly, many couples entering into marriage are not sufficiently prepared, trained or counseled. We all must understand that a Catholic marriage is permanent. Only in certain circumstances does the church declare a marriage "null."

Everyone knows people who have been divorced—maybe even their parents or themselves. As a priest with thirty years of experience as a military chaplain and another fifteen years working in parishes, I've had my share of witnessing Catholic couples getting divorced for almost any reason. Certainly the media, the movies and society as a whole encourage divorce. Another factor in the number of divorces is that we Catholics are not preparing well enough for this most serious of commitments. This lack of preparation for marriage often contributes to an unwillingness to make sacrifices and seek counseling. Instead, when marriage gets tough, some spouses seek the "easy" way out.

Application

Be slow in making commitments. Learn to discern exactly what true love is. True love requires a true understanding of the responsibilities of marriage and family life. If you are considering making a commitment to marry, discuss your concerns and thoughts with your chaplain. Pray for guidance in discerning what is best for you.

Personal Notes:

HAIL MARY

✦ ✦ ✦ ✦ ✦

"Do not be afraid, Mary, for you have found favor with God.
And now, you will conceive in your womb and bear a son,
and you will name him Jesus...." Mary said to the angel,
"How can this be, since I am a virgin?" The angel said to
her, "The Holy Spirit will come upon you, and the power of
the Most High will overshadow you; therefore the child to
be born will be holy; he will be called Son of God."

—LUKE 1:30–31, 34–35

Meditation

Hail Mary full of grace! The Lord is with you; blessed
are you among women, and blessed is the fruit of your
womb, Jesus. Holy Mary, Mother of God, pray for us
sinners, now and at the hour of our death. Amen.

While saying this prayer, reflect on the content of
the Scripture quote. You may even want to read more
of the above passage.

Bishop Fulton Sheen was a very popular TV personality in
the 1950s. Every Sunday thousands would watch his pro-
gram. He told a story about a young couple planning to
get married who came to him for premarriage instruc-
tions. They asked him about the prayer of the rosary and
how monotonous it seemed to repeatedly say the Hail

Mary. Bishop Sheen asked the young man if he loved his fiancée, to which the young man replied, "Certainly, of course!" "When did you last tell her that you loved her?" the bishop asked him. "Why, just before I rang your doorbell." "And before that?" asked the bishop. "While we were driving here," he said. Sheen continued, "Do you think it's monotonous to repeatedly tell her you love her?" The young couple got the point. We never tire of hearing "I love you." So it is with Mary, our heavenly mother.

Application

Repeat the Hail Mary and see whether you can say it with love. The Catholic chaplain can usually provide you with a rosary and even teach you how to pray it. It is comforting to know that our heavenly mother is so close when we are far away from our own friends and family. To find Web sites with other Catholic prayers, search the Internet with the key words "traditional Catholic prayers" or search Amazon.com and AmericanCatholic.org for Catholic prayer books. Also, see the prayers on pages 55-57 in this booklet.

Personal Notes:

PRAYER

. . . . .

And whenever you pray, do not be like the hypocrites; for they love to stand and pray in the synagogues and at the street corners, so that they may be seen by others. Truly I tell you, they have received their reward. But whenever you pray, go into your room and shut the door and pray to your Father who is in secret; and your Father who sees in secret will reward you.

—MATTHEW 6:5–6

Meditation

Take a few minutes meditating on the Scripture passage or continue reading the rest of this passage, which includes the Lord's Prayer (Matthew 6:9–13).

Parade magazine carried an article on prayer citing dozens of studies which reveal that individuals who pray and attend religious services stay healthier and live longer than those who rarely or never do. Dr. Harold Koenig, director of the Duke Center for the Study of Religion, Spirituality and Health at Duke University, states that "prayer boosts morale, lowers agitation, loneliness and life dissatisfaction and enhances the ability to cope in men, women, the elderly, the young, the healthy and the sick." Other physicians state that the power of prayer is too compelling to ignore. The article continues with a quote from Khalita Jones, founder of HE CARES, a spiritually-based organization for the chronically ill (she herself lives with illness): "I couldn't get through a day without prayer."

Application

It's not surprising that, in spite of polls and many studies favoring the value of prayer, there are always skeptics. Yet some of these same people believe in mental telepathy and séances to communicate with the dead. Why is it harder to believe that there is a Supreme Being who will listen to us if we make an effort to talk, communicate and pray to God from our hearts? How have you experienced the power of prayer?

Personal Notes:

BE PREPARED

* * * * *

But about that day and hour no one knows, neither the angels of heaven, nor the Son, but only the Father. For as the days of Noah were, so will be the coming of the Son of Man. For as in those days before the flood they were eating and drinking, marrying and giving in marriage, until the day Noah entered the ark, and they knew nothing until the flood came and swept them all away, so too will be the coming of the Son of Man.

—MATTHEW 24:36–39

Meditation

Take a few minutes to grasp the message of the above quote. No one knows when his or her end will come. Can you say that you would be prepared for the end?

An Iraqi missile launch is detected and its projected impact point is very near to where your unit is located. Someone has been monitoring the FBCB2 computer terminal and has seen the message from division head-quarters. "MOPP4! MOPP4!" someone began shouting. Everyone scrambles for their "mission oriented protec-tive" gear and gets into a shelter and waits. After some time the "all clear" sign is given and everyone breathes easier. Thank God for this modern technology.

Application

I would like to think that God has used technology from the time of creation. The Bible repeatedly warns us to be prepared. Our conscience is our FBCB2 computer. How do you rate your state of preparedness? What do you still need to do to be prepared?

Personal Notes:

SOUND ADVICE

* * * * *

As God's chosen ones, holy and beloved, clothe yourselves with compassion, kindness, humility, meekness,
and patience. Bear with one another and, if anyone has
a complaint against another, forgive each other; just as
the Lord has forgiven you, so you also must forgive.
Above all, clothe yourselves with love, which binds
everything together in perfect harmony.

—COLOSSIANS 3:12–14

Meditation

Take a few minutes to think about the above
passage. It almost sounds like the advice we may
have received from parents.

Fernando Suarez de Solar had emigrated from Mexico
with his family and settled in Southern California. One
of his sons, Jesús, went through school close to Camp
Pendleton, a large training base for the U.S. Marines.
This may have influenced Jesús to join the marines upon
graduating. His family and friends were proud of him,
but his father especially so. Jesús was showing his
gratitude for living in this country. Fernando e-mailed
his son often after he was shipped with his unit to Iraq.
Here is a part of one such message: "I don't want to, nor

dare to, offer an opinion of this war. If it's well-founded or not.... Jesús, my son, I want to tell you so many things that filled my head and heart. I want you to remember, above all, the moral values you inherited from your Hispanic roots and the respect of others. Above all, always remember that you are not an assassin: Be disciplined; don't abuse the enemy, but don't be a coward either. Be firm, but not merciless; don't take advantage of a person who is weak, even if he is the enemy. Be a humanitarian; always help your fallen companions and help the injured, no matter what side they are on." Shortly after Mr. de Solar sent this, two officers came to his door to report that his son was killed.

Application

No matter what branch of service you are in, no matter whether you are male or female, remember that there are people back home who love you and appreciate all the sacrifices you are making for our freedom. Parents, siblings, relatives and friends and even many strangers care for you and wish you well. Know that they are always thinking about you, even when they can't stay in touch or pray for your well-being. How do you respond to those loved ones and strangers who offer words and acts of support and encouragement?

Personal Notes:

BE ALL THAT YOU CAN BE

* * * * *

A dispute also arose among them as to which one of them was to be regarded as the greatest. But he said to them, "The kings of the Gentiles lord it over them; and those in authority over them are called benefactors. But not so with you; rather the greatest among you must become like the youngest, and the leader like one who serves."

—LUKE 22:24–26

Meditation

"Be all that you can be" was once the U.S. Army slogan, and a popular one. Of course, it was a recruiting gimmick, but it challenged young men and women to accept the challenge, to fulfill their dreams of greatness—to join the army. We Catholics must always reach for the stars, to reach for our potential, remembering that we are still mere creatures of God.

Every boxing aficionado has heard and admired the potential of Oscar de la Hoya. He came from humble beginnings but had tremendous energy and developed many of his talents. He has dabbled in acting, singing and golf, but more importantly he has never forgotten his humble beginnings. He has helped young people through charity drives. He also funded a boxing gym to encourage young people to develop physically and avoid the streets. De la Hoya's influence in Southern California, especially in parishes with large Hispanic communities, is powerful. He has led by example.

Application

We don't have to be star athletes or celebrities. What is important is that we recognize the capabilities and talents we have and develop them as best we can. We are all unique creations of God, with human potential and dignity. What are your unique capabilities and talents? How do you share them? How do you lead by example?

Personal Notes:

THE PEOPLE OF GOD

* * * * *

The earth is the Lord's and all that is in it,
        the world, and those who live in it;
for he has founded it on the seas,
        and established it on the rivers.

Who shall ascend the hill of the Lord?
        And who shall stand in his holy place?
Those who have clean hands and pure hearts,
        who do not lift up their souls to what is false,
        and do not swear deceitfully.
They will receive blessing from the Lord,
        and vindication from the God of their salvation.

—PSALM 24:1–5

Meditation

Even when we feel most alone, we are still members
of a team—our unit, our division, our family, our
community and the great family of God. What we
do is important to a lot of people.

The astronauts on the space shuttle *Columbia* were true
heroes representing different parts of the world, different
backgrounds and different religious beliefs. They came
from India, from war-torn Israel and from different parts
of our own country, but they had a single mission for

NASA. They underwent rigorous training, slept in cramped tents, carried sixty-five-pound backpacks, learned about each other's families and established perfect camaraderie. There were no barriers—political, national or religious. They were a *team*. Rick Husband, William McCool, Kalpana Chawla, David Brown, Michael Anderson, Laurel Clark and Ilan Ramon were tremendously accomplished as individuals, but their talents were multiplied by serving with one another. When President George W. Bush was notified of the shuttle disaster and the deaths of these astronauts, he called each of their families to offer his condolences. In his address to the nation he said, "The same Creator who names the stars also knows the names of the seven souls we mourn today. The crew of the shuttle *Columbia* did not return safely to Earth, yet we can pray that all are safely home."

Application

Each of us brings strengths and weaknesses and our own unique history to our military team. Try to learn more about your comrades and strive to become part of a team that is greater than the sum of its members. What are some of the simple and more complex ways you live and work as a team daily? How does each team member contribute to the mission?

Personal Notes:

DON'T BLAME GOD

✦   ✦   ✦   ✦   ✦

Why do you contend against him,
        saying, "He will answer none of my words"?
For God speaks in one way,
…
that he may turn them aside from their deeds,
        and keep them from pride….

—JOB 33:13–14a, 17

Meditation

Take a few moments to reflect on this chapter of
Job in the Old Testament. We humans are so prone
to blame God for anything that goes wrong in our
life or in the lives of those we love, but we seldom
think about the good that comes from God.

Christian evangelist Billy Graham's daughter was inter-
viewed after the September 11, 2001, terrorist attacks.
A reporter asked her, "How could God let something like
this happen?" Anne Graham gave a superb reply, "I
believe," she said, "that God is deeply saddened by this,
just as we are, but for years we've been telling God to
get out of our schools, to get out of our government
and to get out of our lives…. And, being the gentleman
he is, I believe he has calmly backed out. How can we

expect God to give us his blessing and his protection if we demand he leave us alone?"

Application

First and foremost, we must all realize that God has given us a wonderful gift—our free will. How we use it depends entirely on us. Natural disasters or unexpected deaths are the results of weather changes, illnesses and wars. God may allow these things to happen, but God is certainly not the cause. When in your life have you blamed God for something terrible that happened? When have you thanked God for the good things in life?

Personal Notes:

PRAYING FOR ETS

* * * * *

[S]ince the day we heard it, we have not ceased praying for you and asking that you may be filled with the knowledge of God's will in all spiritual wisdom and understanding, so that you may lead lives worthy of the Lord, fully pleasing to him, as you bear fruit in every good work and as you grow in the knowledge of God. May you be made strong with all the strength that comes from his glorious power, and may you be prepared to endure everything with patience, while joyfully giving thanks to the Father, who has enabled you to share in the inheritance of the saints in the light.

—COLOSSIANS 1:9–12

Meditation

One of the most joyful times for soldiers preparing to return to civilian life is his or her ETS, separation from service. Not everyone is a "lifer," so after serving one's country the thought of returning home is exhilarating. What is important for the individual is that he or she must be prepared for changes. The training, the life away from home, the discipline and the maturing are all factors to recognize before shedding the uniform.

Seaman Janet Mutter was a naïve eighteen-year-old when she volunteered for the navy, just after graduating from high school. She had been brought up as a practicing Catholic with good morals. Like any other young person, she went through homesickness, dislike of discipline, and influences good and bad. Somehow Janet stuck to her beliefs and avoided the serious temptations that surrounded her. With the discipline she matured physically, emotionally and psychologically. She took advantage of the educational center located on base and learned to balance her checkbook and establish a regular savings plan. She mingled with other young people whom she met in the chapel youth group. When her time came for separation from the service, she had already been accepted into a prestigious college. She had saved enough to cover the deposit for her tuition. Her parents recognized how much of a beautiful young mature person she had become. She has since entered a convent in San Diego.

Application

Someday you too will be looking forward to ETS. Prepare yourself as much as you can. Develop physically, emotionally and spiritually. Even if the military is not your lifelong career, it can prepare you for the vocation of your choice. Jot down some of your dreams and ambitions for civilian life. What do you need to do to make these dreams become reality and to realize your ambitions?

Personal Notes:

TAPS

* * * * *

But we do not want you to be uninformed, brothers and sisters, about those who have died, so that you may not grieve as others do who have no hope. For since we believe that Jesus died and rose again, even so, through Jesus, God will bring with him those who have died. For this we declare to you by the word of the Lord, that we who are alive, who are left until the coming of the Lord, will by no means precede those who have died. For the Lord himself, with a cry of command, with the archangel's call and with the sound of God's trumpet, will descend from heaven, and the dead in Christ will rise first.

—1 THESSALONIANS 4:13–16

Meditation

In the military we face many risks. The stark fact is that death will come to every human being. Take a few minutes to reflect on the topic of death. Since we cannot avoid it forever, we must prepare for it as best we can.

We've all heard of "Taps," those haunting notes played by a bugler at military funerals. There is a legend about its origin during Civil War days. Union officer Robert Ellicombe came across a dying Confederate soldier and knelt down to try to ease the young soldier's pain. Turning him over, Ellicombe was shocked to see that it was his very own son. Beside himself, the father asked permission of his superiors to hold a military funeral for his son. Hesitatingly (since he was, after all, an enemy soldier), they allowed only one musician, who turned out to be a bugler. Captain Ellicombe had found a piece of paper in his son's pocket. It contained a number of odd-sounding notes, haunting notes. Nonetheless, wishing to honor his son, the father had the bugler play those notes, what we now call "Taps."

Application

What do you think of or how do you feel when you hear "Taps"? Having faith in God and his Son perhaps we can be comforted in knowing that God will certainly take care of us and that Jesus Christ will certainly be at our side when our time comes, we might also remember to pray for the soldiers in whose honor it is played. Whenever you hear "Taps," say a prayer for any comrades known and unknown who have made the ultimate sacrifice in the service of our country.

Personal Notes:

_____

_____

_____

_____

_____

BE MINDFUL ALWAYS

* * * * *

Then Jesus cried aloud: "Whoever believes in me believes not in me but in him who sent me. And whoever sees me sees him who sent me. I have come as light into the world, so that everyone who believes in me should not remain in the darkness."

—JOHN 12:44–46

Meditation

Faith is a mysterious gift. Saint Paul described it as "the evidence of things unseen." Not only does faith give us the power to believe in an unseen God, but it also gives us the light to see other things in a new way. The eyes of faith are a powerful resource.

A young soldier was in his bunkhouse all alone one quiet Sunday morning in Afghanistan. The soldier knew it was Sunday, the holiest day of the week. He took out a deck of cards and laid them out across his bunk. Just then a sergeant came in and said, "Why aren't you with the rest of the platoon?"

The soldier replied, "I thought I would stay behind and spend some time with the Lord."

The sergeant said, "Looks like you are going to play cards."

"No, sir, you see, since we are not allowed to have Bibles or other spiritual books in the country, I've decided to talk to the Lord by studying this deck of cards." The sergeant asked in disbelief, "How will you do that?"

"The ace, Sergeant, reminds me that there is only one God. The two represents the two parts of the Bible, Old and New Testaments. The three represents the Father, Son and the Holy Spirit. The four stands for the four apostles: Matthew, Mark, Luke and John. The five is for the five virgins that were ten but only five of them were glorified. The six is for the six days it took God to create the heavens and earth. The seven is for the day God rested after working the six days. The eight is for the family of Noah and his wife, their three sons and their wives whom God saved from the flood that destroyed the earth for the first time. The nine is for the lepers that Jesus cleansed of leprosy. He cleansed ten, but nine never thanked him. The ten represents the Ten Commandments that God handed down to Moses on the tablets made of stone. The jack is a reminder of Satan. One of God's first angels, he got kicked out of heaven for his wicked ways and is now the ruler of hell. The queen stands for the Virgin Mary. The king stands for Jesus who is the king of all kings. When I count the dots on the cards, I come up with 365 total, one for each day of the year. There are a total of fifty-two cards in a deck; each is a week, fifty-two weeks in a year. So when I talk to God and thank him, I just pull out this old deck of cards and they remind me of all that I have to be thankful for."

The sergeant just stood there. After a minute, with tears in his eyes and pain in his heart, he said, "Soldier, can I borrow that deck of cards?"

Application

Nothing—a cold beer, a deck of cards, your M-16—is good or evil all by itself. It's the way we choose to use things that makes our actions good or bad. Be mindful of how you use the things in your environment. Are you using them to their highest purpose?

Personal Notes:

WOMEN IN COMBAT

* * * * *

There is no longer Jew or Greek, there is no longer slave
or free, there is no longer male and female; for all of
you are one in Christ Jesus.

—GALATIANS 3:28

Meditation

We must learn to accept the fact that it takes people
of both sexes, of all colors, different political beliefs
or religious beliefs to form our powerful military
whose mission is to free the oppressed.

In the early phase of Operation Iraqi Freedom, we read
about female soldiers sacrificing their lives. We came to
know P.F.C. Lori Piestewa, a Hopi Indian and single
mother of two children. On our television screens we
repeatedly witnessed the face of Specialist Shoshana
Johnson as she was led onto the helicopter to freedom.
We witnessed also the rescue of P.F.C. Jessica Lynch by
Special Operations soldiers. What made these stories
different? These were female soldiers who acted no
differently than their male counterparts in similar
circumstances. As a nation, however, we're not used to
seeing women in combat. This novelty is sure to fade
with time, though, because there are thousands of brave

young women who have volunteered to serve out of love of God and country.

Application

Whether you are male or female serving in the military, you must have a deep respect for your fellow soldiers. Gender should not cause you to discriminate among your comrades-in-arms, any more than race or religion. Make an effort to show respect to all others who have chosen to serve, just as you have. Stand up for those who are mistreated by fellow service members.

Personal Notes:

HAVING TO STAY BEHIND

* * * * *

No one has greater love than this, to lay down one's life for one's friends. You are my friends if you do what I command you. I do not call you servants any longer, because the servant does not know what the master is doing; but I have called you friends, because I have made known to you everything that I have heard from my Father. You did not choose me but I chose you.

—JOHN 15:13–16

Meditation

Most soldiers make close friendships in basic training. When forced to separate because of assignments, it is tough to forget those ties. It's worse when we have to stay behind while our buddies are deployed, especially when they are going into combat. We must remember that there is a reason that we fight, not just for our families and our country, but for one another.

I meet with retired and active duty chaplains once a week for dinner and camaraderie. When units of all branches were being deployed to Iraq, the chaplains went with them. This was quite evident when a good number of our active-duty priests did not show up for our gatherings. The active-duty chaplains remaining behind wished they were deploying too, and we retired folks wished we were back in the service. We felt left out. But we all knew that we were still able to support those deployed by performing our duties better, by praying for those in danger and by being appreciative of our freedom.

Application

If you are ever in a situation in which your friends are deploying while you stay behind, remember that you can still do your share back home. The military is like the individual strands of a rope. All the strands together make the rope strong. What can you do to support those comrades who have been deployed?

Personal Notes:

STAND AND BE COUNTED

. . . . .

The LORD is king; let the peoples tremble!
>   He sits enthroned upon the cherubim; let the
>   earth quake!
The LORD is great in Zion;
>   he is exalted over all the peoples.
Let them praise your great and awesome name.
>   Holy is he!
Mighty King, lover of justice,
>   you have established equity;
you have executed justice
>   and righteousness in Jacob.
Extol the LORD our God;
>   worship at his footstool.
>   Holy is he!

—PSALM 99:1–5

Meditation

This part of Psalm 99 chants the greatness of God as seen on Mount Sinai. The psalmist acknowledges God's love for his own chosen people. We too are God's chosen.

Qualcomm Stadium in San Diego, California, is home to the San Diego Chargers football team. One long weekend in 2003, it was home to the evangelist Billy Graham and over 270,000 people, young and old. One guest speaker was a former pro-football place-kicker for the Chargers, Rolf Benirschke. At the age of twenty-four he was diagnosed with a rare intestinal disease. In his book *Alive and Kicking* he explains how the possibility of dying forced him to look at his life and the purpose of his existence. He overcame his illness enough to continue playing football; however, he still felt a void in his life, and finally acknowledged that there was more to life than football. His illness was a blessing because it turned him to accepting his Lord and Savior. It was at Billy Graham's mission that Rolf came forward to be counted.

Application

It is only when we look at life as temporary and the hereafter as eternal that we see what really matters: accepting Jesus and following him wherever he leads us. How can you accept Jesus as Lord and Savior? How can you set a Christian example that others will want to follow?

Personal Notes:

FORGIVING OTHERS

* * * * *

[W]hen you are offering your gift at the altar, if you remember that your brother or sister has something against you, leave your gift there before the altar and go; first be reconciled to your brother or sister, and then come and offer your gift.

—MATTHEW 5:23–24

Meditation

Because of our pride we find it hard to be reconciled to others, especially if they have offended us. Beg God for the grace to work for reconciliation with others.

While on vacation in Naples, Italy, I was enjoying a Sunday morning walk before Mass when a young man brushed up against me and jerked the wristwatch I was wearing off my arm, but not before I had kicked him in the groin, hit him with my clenched fist and cursed at him as he ran up a narrow street. Later, as I knelt in the pew, I was seething with anger and hoping to find the thief. Suddenly I remembered I was to receive Communion. I asked for forgiveness (and prayed I wouldn't confront the thief, in order not to lose my temper again). It worked!

My time in church helped me cool off and realize that the thief held nothing personal against me. It was the watch he wanted. I decided to make a claim to my insurance company for the loss. Restoring peace to my soul was far more important, and as I received the Eucharist, I was able to forgive the thief and pray that he would find honest work.

Application

Forgiving others for intended and unintentional offenses is difficult. It takes all of our courage and humility and our ability to let go. When have you forgiven someone and when have you sought forgiveness?

Personal Notes:

FACING DANGER

* * * * *

Though an army encamp against me,
    my heart shall not fear;
though war rise up against me,
    yet I will be confident.

—PSALM 27:3

Meditation

Veterans of any conflict or war will vouch that war is hell. Anyone serving in the military may have to risk his or her life. The psalmist knew this and called upon God to help. So should we.

Lieutenant J.G. Everett Alvarez, Jr., a navy pilot, was shot down on August 5, 1964, and imprisoned in Hanoi, North Vietnam, on August 11. He relates that while in prison he sketched a cross and conducted his daily church service before that cross. His captors attempted to wear down his spirits. He feared that he might not last. One day he fell down before his cross and began praying fervently. He says that instantly he felt a calm, a peace. He no longer felt afraid.

Application

The perseverance and courage of Alvarez and other American POWs in the "Hanoi Hilton" finally forced the prison commander to allow the prisoners to hold church services. Would your faith in God give you the determination to pray under such difficult circumstances? How can you use your faith to overcome and endure obstacles and hardship?

Personal Notes:

DIFFICULT TIMES

* * * * *

Listen to the sound of my cry,
>   my King and my God,
>   for to you I pray.
O LORD, in the morning you hear my voice;
>   in the morning I plead my case to you, and
>   watch.

—PSALM 5:2–3

Meditation

When we are not at peace within ourselves, we tend to look for someone to blame or complain to. This is a time to pick up the Bible and read.

A daughter was telling her mom how everything was going wrong. She was failing algebra, her boyfriend broke up with her and her best friend was moving out of town. Busy making a cake, her mother asked her if she would like a snack. The daughter replied, "Absolutely, Mom, you know how I love your cakes." "Here, have some cooking oil." "Yuck," said the girl. "How about a few raw eggs?" "Gross, Mom." "Would you like some flour then? Or some baking soda?" "Mom, those things are all yucky!" to which the mother replied, "Yes, all those things seem really bad by themselves. But when they are put together in the right way, they make a delicious cake. God works the same way. Many times we wonder why God lets us go through difficult times. But God knows that when he puts these things in order, they always work for the good. We just have to trust God and eventually things work out for the better. God is crazy about you. Just take the time to talk to him. He will listen."

Application

Think of all the hundreds of times you were disappointed in something that happened to you, or the many times that you wanted something badly. As time passed, and you looked back at the disappointment, it no longer seemed to be a catastrophe. In fact, we often later thank God for answering our prayers with "no." Prayer is not about getting what we want, but getting what's best for us and developing the understanding to see the difference. What do you pray for today?

Personal Notes:

CATHOLIC PRAYERS

* * * * *

Sign of the Cross

In the name of the Father, and of the Son, and of the Holy Spirit. Amen.

The Lord's Prayer

Our Father, who art in heaven, hallowed be thy name. Thy kingdom come, thy will be done, on earth as it is in heaven. Give us this day our daily bread and forgive us our trespasses, as we forgive those who trespass against us. And lead us not into temptation, but deliver us from evil. Amen.

The Hail Mary

Hail Mary, full of grace! The Lord is with thee. Blessed art thou among women and blessed is the fruit of thy womb, Jesus. Holy Mary, Mother of God, pray for us sinners, now and at the hour of our death. Amen.

For the Military

Lord of hosts, bless all who serve our country in the cause of peace on land and sea, and in the air. Help them to meet all danger with courage; let them be models of discipline and loyalty. Amen.

For Those on Orders to Deploy

Heavenly Father, inspire those who are overseas for the cause of peace. Send your Son, Jesus Christ, as the Prince of Peace. Bless the men and women of our military who respond to the needs of peacekeeping. Keep them safe from harm. Let them be models of discipline and courage, and bring them home safely to their loved ones. We ask this in your name. Amen.

Peace Prayer of Saint Francis

Lord, make me an instrument of your peace. Where there is hatred, let me sow love; where there is injury, pardon; where there is doubt, faith; where there is despair, hope; and where there is sadness, joy. O Divine Master, grant that I may not so much seek to be consoled as to console; to be understood as to understand; to be loved as to love. For it is in giving that we receive; it is in pardoning that we are pardoned; and it is in dying that we are born to eternal life.

Act of Contrition

O my God, I am truly sorry for having offended you in thought, word or deed. I dread the loss of heaven and the pains of hell, but even more I regret not thinking of you during times of temptation. I firmly resolve, with the help of your grace, to confess my sins, to do penance and to amend my life. Amen.

Act of Faith, Hope and Love

My God, I believe that you are the one true God in three divine persons; I believe in the birth, death and resurrection of your divine Son, Jesus Christ; that he died for our sins and that he will judge us at the end of the world according to our works. I believe in the Holy Spirit, who continues to teach us the will of the Father and the words of Jesus through the holy Catholic Church. Heavenly Father, trusting in your goodness and mercy, I hope for the forgiveness of sins, the continuing help of your grace and eternal life with you and all those I have loved. Amen.

CONTACTS

Name   Phone

E-mail

Name   Phone

E-mail

Name   Phone

E-mail

Name   Phone

E-mail

Name   Phone

E-mail

Name   Phone

E-mail

Name   Phone

E-mail

Name   Phone

E-mail

Name Phone

E-mail

Name Phone

E-mail

Name Phone

E-mail

Name Phone

E-mail

Name Phone

E-mail

Name Phone

E-mail

Name Phone

E-mail

Name Phone

E-mail

Name

Phone

E-mail

Name

Phone

E-mail

Name

Phone

E-mail

Name

Phone

E-mail

Name

Phone

E-mail

Name

Phone

E-mail

Name

Phone

E-mail

Name

Phone

E-mail